A Joy to Shout About

Messages of Hope and Inspiration

Lucian Rudd

CROSSBOOKS

CrossBooks™
A Division of LifeWay
1663 Liberty Drive
Bloomington, IN 47403
www.crossbooks.com
Phone: 1-866-879-0502

©2010 Lucian Rudd. All rights reserved.

No part of this book may be reproduced, stored in a retrieval system, or transmitted by any means without the written permission of the author.

First published by CrossBooks 11/24/2010

ISBN: 978-1-6150-7670-3 (sc)
ISBN: 978-1-6150-7671-0 (dj)

Library of Congress Control Number: 2010941133

Printed in the United States of America

This book is printed on acid-free paper.

Any people depicted in stock imagery provided by Thinkstock are models, and such images are being used for illustrative purposes only.

Certain stock imagery © Thinkstock.

Because of the dynamic nature of the Internet, any Web addresses or links contained in this book may have changed since publication and may no longer be valid. The views expressed in this work are solely those of the author and do not necessarily reflect the views of the publisher, and the publisher hereby disclaims any responsibility for them.

Dedicated to Betty
My Beloved Wife
For her
Patience and Support

Meet the Author

Lucian Rudd has been in the ministry for fifty nine years, serving in churches in Missouri, Iowa and Texas, forty five of those years in the Midland/Odessa, Texas area. For six of those years he owned and operated Christian bookstores in Midland, Odessa and San Angelo, Texas.

He grew up in Port Arthur, Texas, and then moved on to college at Hardin-Simmons University in Abilene, Texas, and Southwestern Baptist Theological Seminary in Fort Worth, Texas. He served in student pastorates near Fort Worth, Texas, followed by full-time pastorates in Missouri and Iowa, then back to Texas, settling in the Odessa-Midland area of west Texas in the middle 1960s. He was pastor of Belmont Baptist Church, Odessa, at the time these messages were originally developed and broadcast

Since retirement he has preached in churches throughout the area and has served as interim pastor for several. For eleven years he has also worked as a substitute teacher, mainly in the Midland, Texas, high schools.

Email: Lucian2509@Gmail.com
Twitter: www.Twitter.com/lrudd
Facebook: www.Facebook.com/lrudd4
Website: www.LucianRudd.com

Table of Contents

A Joy to Shout About 8
Redeeming the Time 10
Hurry Up! 12
Helping Others 14
Stand Up for Jesus 16
Walking Before God 18
We Can Do You Good! 20
A Living Sacrifice 22
Shining Sun Christian 24
Train Up the Child 26
The Ninety and Nine 28
Sunday for the Lord? 30
Words Can Hurt! 32
Light for Life 34
Got Enough Excitement? 36
Jesus, the Way; the Only Way! 38
See You in Church? 40
A Lesson on Salvation 42
Radical Christians? 44
Serving Others 46
An Answer to Poverty 48
Sorrow is Better than Laughter? 50

We All Depend on One Another 52
Create in Me a New Heart 54
You Can Do It! 56
Count Your Blessings 58
Real Thanks 60
Make a Joyful Noise 62
Success Out of Struggle 64
The Real Meaning of Love 66
What Does Christmas Really Mean? 68
Talk Back to the Preacher 70
The Message of Christmas 72
Is the Church's Message Relevant Today? 74
Stable Ground in a Changing World 76
Jesus, Afflicted and Oppressed for Us 78
God Said 80
Can You Believe? 82
Casual Christian or Deep Dedication? 84
Let No Man Take Your Crown 86
Index of Scriptures 88

Introduction

The preaching of the Word never seems to be out-of-season. Political, economic and social problems always need to be addressed. We need the inspiration and guidance of the Scripture, the proclamation of the mind of God. What is His answer to our needs? What is His call to us to give direction to our lives?

The messges in this book reflect His call for today, even though they were originally prepared and broadcast on radio over forty years ago. Turbulent times were the background then and the same can be said for today.

The messages carried over and printed here are for the purpose of inspiration and support in our times of special need. They come with the hope and prayer that you can be blessed and lifted by them.

Over seventy five (75) scriptures are quoted, referenced or commented on in the text of the book. A scripture index at the back of this book will be helpful in finding the messages where these scriptures are discussed or referenced.

For deeper inspiration and maybe a more life changing experience, check out the BONUS section called The System and see how the messages can mean even more to you. More uses are being developed by the author to be used in Bible study and inspirational groups.

BONUS!!
The System

Here is a suggestion. I call it "The System." In order to get the most meaning from the messages try this method to let them become an inner part of your life. Read them one at a time and repeat your reading for five days or a week. The repetition lets them become more and more grounded in your daily life and lets them become a part of you. Remember how many times we repeated the multiplication tables? Or how many times we have to work with a new computer program or electronic device to really become comfortable with it? Some motivational programs are based largely on listening repeatedly to tapes or cd's, with repitions of five to seven , or even ten times. You will be surprised how something that you had hardly noticed will "jump out" at you after a few repetitions and how much more clearly God can speak to you.

One suggestion for a small study group would be to pick a message to be studied the next week, then assign it to the group members to read once each day for five days to enhance the inspiration level. Then, in the group meeting discuss the inspiration, impowerment and leadership felt by each member, with the goal being to increase the spiritual results. See the website, www.LucianRudd.com for more information, helps and ideas.

**Shout with joy before the Lord!
Come before Him singing with joy.**
Ps 98:4(Living Psalms)

A Joy to Shout About

There is one characteristic of life that should by all means be a part of every Christian personality and that is joy, real, genuine joy, the kind that glows in every element of life's experience. But so often it's missing. Somewhere we have received the impression that spiritual things are so serious that we must have the proper facial expression to fit the mood.

Jesus had a long talk with His disciples one day, and he said, **These things I have spoken to you, that my joy might remain in you and that your joy might be full.** (John 15:11). The prophet Isaiah said, **Therefore with joy shall ye draw water out of the wells of salvation.** (Isaiah 12:3).

It's really simple. The Christian experience is characterized by the joy salvation brings. We speak many times about the responsibilities of the Christian. But the so-called responsibility is service performed out of a feeling of love and thanksgiving for what God has already given.

"Rejoice in the Lord," is the clarion call of the scriptures! God has made us, God has provided for us. When we have trusted in His Son, Jesus Christ; we have life eternal, everlasting joy. God be praised, we have peace because He wipes away all our worries, we have assurance because we know He will take care of us; we stand boldly in the face of bitter opposition because we know He has an eternal home for us in heaven.

There will be trouble in the here and now. There will be hard times. There will be sorrows and bitter battles with temptation. We will often stumble under the load, but through our tears we can still see the glory of our Christ. And, in the pain, we can feel the working of His Holy Spirit as he heals our bruises and blisters.

Certainly, the world is in a terrible shape. We've helped make it that way. The problems and the pressures sometimes become almost unbearable, but beyond it all we have a future -- a heavenly future; and in it all we have peace that is beyond the fondest imagination of our worldly acquaintances.

Glory, hallelujah, we have a joy to shout about!

Redeeming the Time

A prudent man foreseeth the evil, and hideth himself: but the simple pass on, and are punished. (Proverbs 22:3). **The heart of the prudent getteth knowledge.** The Apostle Paul told the Ephesians **See that ye walk circumspectly, not as fools, but as wise. redeeming the time, because the days are evil.** (Ephesians 5:15-16).

The business community of the world has learned that success comes only to those who exercise some ingenuity -- those who are willing to try something new occasionally; those who are willing to use the tools that have been developed to foster business growth and success. The advertising media, computer technology, detailed programming and planning, assembly production methods, and the latest in communication technology are being used to great advantage and profit.

To a great extent, Christendom, and individual Christians, seeking to reach out into the world with the message of Jesus Christ, have not always acted wisely. Often, we used the most primitive of tools, and we abhorred the thought of paying the price for the latest technology. For that reason, many of our children were growing up with better knowledge of the latest jingle advertising coffee, the new cars, or some other product in general use, while they could not quote the simplest scripture verse. For most, more time was spent viewing the action of a wild, beat 'em up brawl in a TV-land tavern each week than was spent in the spiritual, character-building experience of worship each month. For the most part the churches have overcome a lot of this. Better equipment is being used. Sometimes it may even be overused.

If Christianity really has anything to offer the public, it's evident that it needs to present a very convincing story. A lot can be said about this. There are many ideas and attitudes that we must develop to be able to give an effective presentation of the Gospel today. The starting place is *you* (you thought I was talking about *them* didn't you?). Make the vow, now, as you go out into the world, today, that you will live your life as if you're convinced that Christianity is the very best way of life. And be alert to the opportunities that you have, as an individual or as a part of a group, to help in the presentation of the message of Christ in such a way as to get the most message to the greatest number of folks. Jesus said, **The children of this world are in their generation wiser than the children of light.** (Luke16:8). But He said if we have faith we can move mountains! Okay! Let's try!

Hurry Up!

"Y'all hurry up, now!" That word *hurry* certainly describes our world today. It seems that we are always in a rush, dashing here, running there, and flying somewhere else. Maybe it's not so bad to be in a hurry, but often in the hurrying and scurrying, we are at loose ends. Many times, real purpose is missing. People rush to places without knowing what to do when they get there. Many are rushing through the world without actually being aware of what is going on around them. It might be best, sometimes, to move more slowly so that we truly see the people, the things, the conditions that surround us in the here and now.

Consider yourself, your actions, your life. Is it possible that you, too, are hurrying so quickly to some future date or some faraway place that you're not really living today? Job 37:14 says, **Stand still and consider the wondrous works of God.** Isaiah 41:20 says, **That they may see, and know, and consider, and understand together, that the hand of the Lord hath done this.**

Of course, you have dreams, plans, and ambitions. You want to advance in your job, you want success, you want to travel. Maybe plans are already made for that trip of a lifetime, but don't miss out on living today because of what you hope is out in the future Today, come into the presence of God. Live today the love of God as you actually communicate with your surroundings. Look into the faces of the persons around you. What do you see there? Loneliness? Hurt? Fear? Grief? One great privilege that God allows you in life is to be a tool of His grace for others.

God's love is not expressed in great booming proclamations from the heavens. God's help is not expressed so much in supplying needs through great supernatural miracles as it is in the voice and life and action of a person dedicated to live his life as a channel through which God can speak and act.

The one great difference between the person who is rushing to and fro and the person who is living more slowly is the hurrying one is living for himself, rushing to grab life before someone takes it from him. The other is living for others, looking to see human needs around him as well as the beauty of God's universe. Both people can have ambition; both can be going somewhere in life ... but which one will enjoy life the most?

Helping Others

We often miss some of the meanings of the Scripture because we don't take the time to think through what is being said, and therefore we don't apply it to our present-day lives. One such passage is Matthew 25:41-46, which we often fail to apply personally. Dan Crawford of Edinburg, Texas, has written a paraphrase of the message in that passage:

"I was hungry but you were in a hurry to get to your luncheon and fellowship with your friends. I was imprisoned in a ghetto and you came to the mission to play games with my children. I was naked and you went to your study group to discuss the moral implications of my condition. I was thirsty for truth and you passed me by on the way to your formal worship service. I was a lonely stranger in your midst but you were interested in enlisting those you knew. I was sick of sin but your evangelism consisted of maturing your own faith". The student asked, "But Lord, when did we ever see you like this?" The Lord answered back, "I tell you indeed, whenever you refused to help one of these, you refused to help me."

Certainly it would be out of order for us to interpret that the whole of Christian experience is to be judged on a social Gospel approach. We should help others. No, we MUST help others. But there's more to spiritual life than social action. In fact, for social action to be Christian, it absolutely must be so performed that the message of Jesus is proclaimed in word and deed. It should be clearly established that the love of Christ is the underlying motive for the action. Though a Christian may act, his actions must point to Jesus to be Christian.

Now, it is necessary that every Christian will in some way set out to be of definite service to his fellow-man. Each of us can look around just a little and find someone who needs help that we have the ability to render.

You may think that you are the exception. You may think you cannot do anything that will be helpful. But there is no exception! Someone will be looking to you, today. It may be material or it may be spiritual. It may be a big thing or it may seem an insignificant thing. It may require physical effort or just a smile. The one major element in whatever you are called upon to do will be LOVE. Paul said it in Corinthians **Though I bestow all my goods to feed the poor, and though I give my body to be burned, and have not charity, I am nothing**. (1 Corinthians 13:3)

Someone needs your love today. That someone may be poverty stricken, or that someone may be the wealthiest person you know in this world. Still, an open heart and an open mind, motivated by the wonderful love of Jesus Christ, will determine correctly your course of action.

Stand Up for Jesus

It was a great citywide revival campaign in Philadelphia, back in 1858. Preachers from all parts of the nation were leading. But none was more powerful than a youthful Episcopalian, Dudley Tyng. One Sunday morning he stood before 5,000 men in Jayne's Hall. Before he closed the service, one of every five men in the great hall was on his knees in prayer. The middle of the following week, Mr. Tyng moved too close to a corn-shelling machine, a sleeve of his coat caught in the machinery, and his arm was literally torn from his shoulder.

As doctors and ministers gathered at the bedside of the dying Mr. Tyng, he tried to sing "Rock of Ages," but he was too weak. His father leaned close to hear his last words, and the dynamic young minister faintly whispered, "Tell them to stand up for Jesus."

The scene so impressed George Duffield, Jr., a Presbyterian minister, that his next sermon was from the text; **Stand therefore, having your loins girt about with truth.** (Ephesians 6:14). For the conclusion of his sermon, he composed and read a poem. Someone had the verse printed on leaflets for use in Sunday School. One of the leaflets found its way to a Baptist Periodical. Six years later, Mr. Duffield was visiting Union army camps and heard soldiers singing the poem he had written, he didn't even know he had written a hymn, a hymn inspired by the last words of a dying minister.

Stand up; stand up for Jesus, Ye soldiers of the cross;
Lift high his royal banner, it must not suffer loss:

We still sing it today in our worship services .. and it remains relevant. You and I are in open conflict with the powers of sin. If the battle is to be won, we must in truth STAND UP FOR JESUS. How will you do it today? How will you face the powers of evil? How will you magnify Jesus Christ? It depends altogether on your personality, on the problems and temptations that arise, on the elements of evil that will confront you, on many things. But remember this, you will be asked to give an answer. yes or no. You will be asked to take a side in a discussion, an action, and a problem. Somehow, today, you will have the chance to show the world that you really are a Christian, that you really are on the side of good and of God. STAND UP FOR JESUS! HOLD THE BANNER HIGH!

Osbeck, Kenneth, *101 Hymn Stories,* Kregel, Grand Rapids, MI, 1982.

Walking Before God

This is the age of gadgets, of passive entertainment and of wheels. We ride everywhere we go, even to the corner grocery store (if there's still one in your neighborhood). But now the health enthusiasts are telling us that we must do more walking. So, walking, or jogging for the more energetic, is becoming the great health program of the hour. Well, walking has been encouraged throughout the ages, even in the spiritual sense. I have found several scriptures that will point to the kind of walking to which I am referring.

In Genesis 17:1, the Lord says, **I am the almighty God; walk before me, and be thou perfect.** In Leviticus 26:12, He says, **I will walk among you and will be your God.** In the Gospel according to Matthew 14:25, we find Jesus walking on the sea. Also, in John 5:8, when Jesus had performed a healing miracle, **He said, Rise, take up thy bed and walk.**

But let's concern ourselves with our own walking, yours and mine. We are to walk before God, with an attempt to be perfect, righteous. Let's remember that whether we may realize it or not, we walk before the Lord all of the time... He sees and knows our every move, even our thoughts. Several things can be said about our walking.

First, Paul said in Ephesians 5:2, **Walk in love.** That is, walk in an attitude and spirit of love for God and love for men. Love is an outpouring concern for the well being of others. Walk, or live daily, with this genuine concern for the best in the lives of those who live around you.

Second, in Ephesians 5:8, Paul said, **Walk as children of light.** A child of light in the scripture is a person who has come from the darkness of sin into the light of salvation, having met Jesus Christ and having trusted in His redeeming work of Calvary for eternal life. When you are a child of light you don't hide your life actions, you live openly, showing the persons with whom you have contact that Jesus has come into your life.

Third, again from Paul's comments in Ephesians 5:15, **See then that ye walk circumspectly, not as fools, but as wise.** In other words, pay attention to what is going on around you - don't stumble into temptation because of carelessness. Recognize that Satan will use every device possible to ruin your Christian witness. Stay alert, watch where you're going so you won't get backed into a corner.

So, while you are walking to tighten those muscles or take those pounds off, think also about the spiritual walk – walk in love, walk like a Christian, walk wisely.

We Can Do You Good!

As the Hebrew people journeyed on their way from Egypt to the land which God had promised them, Moses extended an invitation to his brother-in-law**, Come thou with us, and we will do thee good**. (Numbers 10:29) This is the message and invitation of Christians to the world today. We may have a little difficulty in saying it sometimes because of our many faults. We may be a little self-conscious in saying it because it sounds so much like bragging; but the truth is that this is a fact and that it is a part of God's plan for the ages. Anytime a Christian can draw a person of the world out of the grips of sin into the eternal relationship of the family of God ... the Christian is doing the person good.

Maybe we'd better look at a few more of the words in that verse in Numbers 10, **Come with us and we will do you good: <u>for the Lord hath spoken good concerning Israel.</u>** Israel is a type of the kingdom of God, the chosen people of God. God has, in fact, spoken well concerning his people, the people who have trusted in his son, Jesus Christ. If you are a Christian, you can make the invitation with full confidence for God has indeed spoken well about you.

He has redeemed you, he has given you eternal life. He has stood at your side to help you in time of trouble and to guide you in time of special need. He has made special plans for you for all of eternity. He has given you a place in his kingdom.

You and your church can invite others to come along with you and you can promise to do them good as long as you seek to learn and live the wonderful truths of the Word of God. Too many times Christians and churches are self-conscious about their failing and sin, but an earnest desire and honest seeking for the Lord's will can take care of the problem.

Okay! So you have problems! Don't you think God can take care of them for you? Didn't the Hebrew people have problems? Sure they did! They even wanted to go on back to Egypt to be slaves, again. They were ready to just throw up their hands and quit, but in the end, God led them right into the promised land. And eventually, through them, He gave the world its wonderful Savior.

If you have a problem with your own life, bow your head, now, and ask God to forgive you and help you to do better, then get up and go tell someone how wonderful your savior is and invite them to come along life's way with you, for you and the Lord can do them good. It's good to be a Christian. It's good to know Jesus. It's good to be able to say, "Come on with us, we can do you good!"

A Living Sacrifice

Greater Love hath no man than this, that a man lay down his life for his friends. (John 15:13) You have heard this verse of scripture many times, I am sure. And the normal response to the passage brings the thought of one dying for his friend. I'm sure that Jesus had that same basic meaning, for He was talking to his disciples about giving his own life on the cross for mankind. But, let me draw your attention a little different direction and let's see another meaning in a man laying down his life for friends.

Romans 12:1 says, **Present your bodies a living sacrifice.** It gives a deeper insight into what I want to say. There is more to giving your life for others than just dying. When you die, that's all of it. Give your life for others in a continuing manner. Maybe we can say it another way, *live* your life for others. Give yourself in personal service and ministry to the needs other people have in life.

Jesus gave His life in death on the cross, but He arose from the grave, ascended into heaven, and prepares a place for us there, today. He lives among us today in the work and ministry of His Holy Spirit. By the same token, He wants you and me to live and work and minister to others as we continue our daily existence among them.

How can you do this? The main way is to live and speak the Gospel, the Good News of Jesus Christ. You don't have to be a great Bible scholar or theologian to do it. You need to know Jesus Christ as your own personal savior and you need to be able to tell others what he has done for you in salvation and in daily sustenance.

It is good to know a few scriptures, but that's not the key. Most of the people you meet in our part of civilization know a few of them, too;

but what they don't know is just how Christ has worked in and through your life to save you and cleanse you from all unrighteousness.

Now let me tell you something. This isn't something that will take a few moments out of your day; this is something that will demand the best out of every moment that you live and breathe. It will demand total submission to the power and leadership of the Holy Spirit. It will demand complete subjection of your life and personality to the consideration of every action and its effect on persons around you.

You will have to love your fellowmen with an endless love and literally die to yourself and selfish desires to give yourself so completely. It will be the hardest thing you ever did – but it will be the greatest! Just do it!

Shining Sun Christian

What kind of person should a Christian be, whether that person be you or me? Should we be different from others in the world? Of course we should! But how should we be different? A quotation of the Scripture, Judges 5:31 can help us, **Let them that love him be as the sun when he go forth in his might.**

Have you ever noticed the beauty and the glory of the sun at noonday? The sunrise is lovely... and so is the sunset, but it's the noonday sun that lights the earth the brightest. May God give us men whose lives reflect the glory of the Savior without any of the shades of darkness!

There is a certain glory in the life of every Christian, some special way that God shows His personality and love. Every personality is different and each life varies from its neighbor. God's dealing with each person is related to an entirely different set of circumstances, but the glory of His forgiveness, the change of character, the new life He has created can shine with magnificent brightness for others to see.

Now, let's be careful with the interpretation, here. I would not even begin to suggest that any degree of pride should be part of this "shining sun" Christian, for pride clouds the personality and reduces the intensity of shining light. In all of life, the Christian says, "Any brightness or glory that I might have in my life is a result of the presence of God, not of any power within myself."

Paul said in Philippians 2:15, **In the midst of a crooked and perverse generation ... ye shine as lights in the world.** Here's the proposition, God wants you to add a special brightness to your surroundings, a spiritual brightness that could best be compared to the brightness of the sun at noonday, a brightness that will reach into the darkest recesses of the souls of friends and acquaintances, brighten their day and give them the light of the Gospel of Jesus Christ, so that they, too, may be drawn into a personal, vital relationship with Him.

Will you do it? Ask God for the strength, the insight, and the personality to brighten the corner where you are, today. You can do it! I know you can, with His help!

Train Up the Child

On several occasions I have read of the destruction of personal property that has taken place on the public streets of the very large cities, and I have thought to myself, "I'm glad I don't live in a place like that." But, you know, the fact was brought home to me some time ago that the evil of wanton destruction and vandalism is everywhere: the big city, the small city, the town, and the open country.

The thing that reminded me of the awfulness of the destruction and its presence in our own city was a car that was left on the street in front of our church. It had a flat tire and the driver left it there several days. Of course, it shouldn't have been left there, abandoned, for that long, but that's not the point. The first couple of nights everything was allright, but the next time I drove by the abandoned car, I was shocked to see that during the night someone had broken every window. As it turned out, I think a teenager owned the car ... and I'm sure he did not have the funds to make the necessary repairs immediately. In all probability there was not sufficient insurance coverage to repair it for him so, you see, for all practical purposes, his prize possession was destroyed. And get this, it all happened on a brightly lighted, well traveled street, across from our church building, in our friendly west Texas city.

Many other illustrations could be cited, but here's my question: What is wrong when things like this take place? Many, if not most, of these things are done by wandering groups of youth at hours when they have no business being out on the streets. Is this telling our generation something? The Bible says, in Proverbs 22:6, **Train up a child in the way he should go: and when he is old, he will not depart from it.**

The growing vandalism rate is telling us that we have not been training up the children the way they should go!

Part of the youth 'problem' of today is also a result of this – rebellion against the carelessness and hypocrisy of adults. Far too many are the parents and guardians who simply do not care what the children are doing – or what kind of adults they become. The youth are crying out, "Show us how to act! Give us some direction! Give us some help!" Christians arise! This is the hour that great need exists. Show the young of our nation and the world that Jesus Christ is the way, the truth, and the life.

The Ninety and Nine

A great revival team was established in 1870 when Ira Sankey and Dwight L. Moody met at a YMCA convention at Indianapolis, Indiana. Sankey was a musician of great talent. He sang, he played the piano and he composed music. He sang solos to his own accompaniment and became the best-known revival song leader in history. An interesting occurrence took place about four years after Sankey and Moody began working together.

They had just finished a revival in Glasgow, Scotland, and were on their way to an engagement in Edinburgh. Moody worked on his correspondence while Sankey read a paper he had bought as they passed through the railroad station.

As Sankey read the paper, he noticed a poem that had been written by an orphan Scottish girl some years before. She had died five years before the Glasgow paper happened to reprint her poem to fill out the page. Ira Sankey tore the poem out of the paper, put it in his pocket and forgot it.

In the Edinburgh revival, Moody preached the first message of the week on the good shepherd. It was time for Sankey's solo, but he had not been told the subject ahead of time, and he had no appropriate selection. Then he thought of the poem in his pocket. The words fit the subject well -- but there was no music for the verses.

He put the newspaper clipping on the music rack, breathed a prayer, started playing and started singing. Those few moments were the "most intense" of his life. Would you believe it? In those moments a hymn tune was composed, note for note, while the composer sang it publicly for the first time!

The congregation was spellbound! When Moody asked him where he had gotten that song, Ira Sankey could only point to the newspaper clipping. Ira Sankey was great, but he was great because he allowed God to use him in a marvelous way just when he was needed.

You can be used by God, too. Maybe not in the same way as Sankey was used, but maybe in an even greater way. How? Place yourself in the complete control of God.

What about that song Ira Sankey composed and played and sang for a live audience? The poem the little girl had written started out like this:

> There were ninety and nine that safely lay
> In the shelter of the fold,
> But one was out on the hills away,
> Far off from the gates of gold.
> Away on the mountain wild and bare,
> Away from the tender shepherd's care.

Clint Bonner, <u>A Hymn is Born</u>: Broadman Press, Nashville, TN, 1959. pg. 121

Sunday for the Lord?

One of the great running battles of past years was the battle of Sunday business. Anytime a stable business, respected through the years, made a move toward opening for business there arose a cry to the very heavens, with threats of boycott. Preachers would shout, editors would pound their holy typewriters to stir up marchers, raise banners and generally cry aloud at the audacity of businesses even thinking of opening their stores on Sunday. And all the time, nothing was said about the hundreds of stores that were already open each and every Sunday... and nothing was said about the thousands and thousands of Christians who were patronizing these businesses on Sunday, yet!

Each Sunday, as I left church, I drove by grocery stores, drug stores, discount houses and even a new car dealership. They were all open for business. And do you know what I saw -- church goers, still in their Sunday best going shopping as if it were any other day of the week.

And I said to myself, "What's wrong with this picture? Where's the problem? Who's at fault?" It's easy to say that the business man is awful, terrible, a disgrace, a money-grabbing evil influence in our society. And, it's sometimes true. It's easy, also, to say the shoppers are wrong, that they shouldn't demand Sunday store hours, that they shouldn't stop and shop on Sundays. But I'm afraid that we will just have to lay part of the blame on our churches. Somewhere, we have missed the point in teaching the sacredness of the Lord's day.

God has made the day for us, and He has so created us that we actually need the day. We need the spiritual filling and the spiritual rest that the day allows. No man is truly happy who does not spend this time to deepen his relationship with his God.

What will we ever do about it? I'm not sure! The major need is a revitalization of the Lord's day in the minds and hearts of all men. Christians should be the first to take a definite stand in the issue, not as much a stand to do battle with the Sunday openers as a stand to definitely refrain from doing business on Sunday, a stand to really remember the Lord's day and keep it holy.

Sunday is a day for special Bible study and for worship. Will you make an honest attempt this week to finish your business before Sunday? And then, spend Sunday with God, in worship, in Bible study, in Christian training, letting Him fill you and strengthen you for continued Christian service and living.

Words Can Hurt!

Here is an interesting Proverb for you today, **Where no wood is, there the fire goeth out: so where there is no talebearer, the strife ceaseth.** (Proverbs 26:20) A modern, paraphrased translation of the same proverb goes like this: **"Without wood a fire goes out, without gossip a quarrel dies down."** (NIV) To paraphrase a number of proverbs, Biblical and secular, "Gossip is a dainty morsel eaten with great relish". Have you ever noticed just how prevalent gossiping and tale-bearing is in our modern world?

Here is an evil that is as senseless as anything you can imagine for most of the gossip is carried by so-called friends. Yes, I really mean it! If you will spend the time to analyze this mouth-driven phenomenon, you will see that most of the hurting stories are told by someone who is a friend of the victim. It always starts, "Did you hear about …? I never would have imagined!" And on it goes. It's only after the tale has been told and you find that it wasn't correct in the first place that you begin to wish you could call back the stories.

Did you hear about the woman who had started a particularly harmful bit of gossip about her neighbor? She found out later how terribly wrong she had been and she asked her pastor how she might undo the gossip she started. The preacher picked up a pillow and asked her to follow him to the porch; he cut a hole in the pillow, emptied the feathers over the porch rail, watched them scatter as a small breeze bore them on its wings; then he turned to her and said, "Will you go out now and gather up everyone of the feathers?" She said, "Why that would be impossible!" He looked at her sorrowfully and replied, "Exactly. So it is with your gossip."

Remember, spoken words cannot be erased. They are borne out on wings of the air and their hurt can move on into infinity. Anytime you are tempted to tell tales on someone, even things that are true, remind yourself of two words that sound similar, but whose meanings are so different. One of them is gossip -- the evil, destructive device of telling things that break down character. The other is gospel -- good news, the wonderful, life-giving, telling of the good news of God through the message of Jesus Christ.

Remember the Proverb 26:20. Tensions disappear when gossip stops. How peaceful it would be and how good would be the news if tale bearing would cease. Join the move for peace! Stop gossip today! Tell, instead, the good news of Christ!

NOTE: I tried to trace the story of the pillow and found that there are untold numbers of stories like it on the internet. Sorry I couldn't get the exact origin. LR.

Light for Life

I said to a man who stood at the gate of the year, "Give me a light that I may tread safely unto the unknown," and he replied, "Go out into the darkness and put your hand into the hand of God. That shall be to you better than a light and safer than a known way." (Haskins). That quotation is strengthened by the words of the Psalmist, "**Unless the Lord had been my help, my soul had almost dwelt in silence.**" (Psalm 94:17). In another place he said, "**I laid me down and slept; I awaked; for the Lord sustained me.**" (Psalm 3:5).

For many of us there is difficulty in going out into the dark unknown of the future. Many circumstances in life call for us to make decisions that change our entire course of life, without any real knowledge of what will lie ahead. We make a desperate effort to obtain security, that something that guarantees us that everything will be alright in days to come, but the stark truth is that security as we imagine it is absolutely impossible to obtain.

The fact is that God gives us the light of life one step at a time. For most of us, if He laid our whole future out before us we would not be able to bear the knowledge. As it is we follow Him step by step and seek to do His will for each day as it comes, and He gives us deepening insight into his ways with man.

As we faithfully follow, God imparts to us a degree of wisdom, little by little. Then with the passage of time we are surprised at the things we have been able to do. Today might be compared to one step in your life-journey. Take hold of the insight that God has given you for today and live your best for Him. It may be just a common day with nothing really different or important, but you can never tell how God will use the common to make way for the glorious. Here's a simple line from Horace that was quoted for centuries (Odes I:xi), "Seize the day." Its meaning is, "Live in the immediate present, since you have no assurance of the future." Let's apply it here. Today is the only day you can be certain about. Live it the very best you can.

Proverbs 16:20 says, **"Whoso trusteth in the Lord, happy is he."** True happiness can be yours when you place your hand in the hand of God and let Him lead you through the darkness of the future, lighting for you each step of the way.

Haskins, Minnie, The Desert, UK, 1908.

Got Enough Excitement?

One of the reasons for the decline and fall of Rome was an almost mad desire for excitement, a desire that led to all sorts of moral extravagances which finally engulfed and helped destroy the great empire. Excitement, thrills, exotic activity, these were the things most searched for. Have you ever thought how close we are in America to the very same attitude?

Look at the sports arena. We have traveled the extreme from good sportsmanship to a "win-at-all-cost" psychology. Gambling is a part of this picture, too, from the office pools on the local school game to the great network of bookies taking bets on games and races and fights throughout the year.

Look at the night-life entertainment. Alcohol flows like water as good time guys and gals get high. And if alcohol won't do the job well enough, then there's always a drug of some kind.

Look at the man and woman relationship. Private illicit affairs are no longer the talk of the town. They are too common. But now the love affairs, illicit or proper, are being replaced by an open bombardment of suggestive sex advertising and by wild sex orgies.

Look, even at the more acceptable area of driving an automobile. No longer can we be satisfied with a good machine that will get us there. It has to have all the trimmings of speed that you can get, and still many of the young drivers are blowing engines trying to make the motorized monsters do still more.

Look at any area of life. For anything to be acceptable it has to be exciting, different, dangerous, and certainly anywhere but dullsvile! Even in our Christian circles the only person who can get the ear of the people is the person who has a real exciting story.

This is frightening. Do you know why? Because a great number of our potentially effective Christians servants are shying away from trying to do something in the name of Christ, either because they cannot see enough excitement in it or because they feel they don't have anything exciting enough to say. There are still others who are being lost to the cause because they are 'trying on' some of the excitement of the world and they are quickly becoming enslaved.

Today is your day! Be careful how you live it. Psalms 112:2 says, **"The generation of the upright shall be blessed"**. And I really believe that. We just don't need all the excitement that the world tries to thrust upon us.

Jesus, the Way; the Only Way!

"We're all striving for the same place. It doesn't matter so much what you believe, just so you believe it and are sincere about it" Dr. Wayne DeHoney heard an oriental princess say the same thing in Honolulu, "Many pathways lead up the mountain. We believe that all who sincerely press on the upward way will eventually arrive at the mountaintop to view the same moonlight together." But, what about the words of Jesus? **"I am the way, the truth and the life; no man cometh to the Father, except by me."** (John.14:6) Or, what about the words of Peter in Acts. 4:12? **"Neither is there salvation in any other: for there is none other name under heaven given among men, whereby we must be saved."**

We're all striving for the same place, maybe, but it certainly does make a difference what we believe. Salvation, eternal life and forgiveness of sin, all depend upon your personal response to the call of Jesus Christ, your relationship to Him. Peter said it well in Acts 10:42,43, He commanded us to preach unto the people, and to testify that it is He which was ordained of God to be the Judge of the quick and the dead. **"To Him give all the prophets witness, that through his name whosoever believeth in him shall receive remission of sins."** When Peter had finished his message, many who heard him were saved that very moment, for they believed in the name of Jesus Christ as Peter had presented him to them.

Now this can be true in your life. You can be forgiven; you can be saved; you can find your way to the top of the mountain. But you must find that way in a vital, personal relationship with the Jesus Christ about whom I speak.

Goodness won't do it. Kindness won't do it. Morality won't do it. Even church attendance and participation won't do it, though it will open you to further influence of the Gospel. Nothing will do it except your exercise of your own will to believe in Christ as Savior and as Lord. When you do this, things won't be the same anymore. You won't live for self. You won't live any longer in an easy-come-easy-go manner. You will live for God, be a messenger of God, a servant of God, a worshipper of God, for, you see, Jesus' life work was to reveal the Father (God) to us so that we might really know Him, love Him and live for Him. Jesus paid the penalty for sin when He died on the cross, and it's our belief in Him and what He did that saves us.

Jesus Christ is the only way up the mountain for you, for me, for everyone!

DeHoney, Wayne, Quoted many places. Unable to trace original.

See You in Church?

Many times we hear complaints about the terrific problems that are part of regular church attendance. The building is too cold or too hot, the Sunday school room is too far from the auditorium, the pews are too hard, the preacher's too loud -- and on and on. You'd think God should issue special medals for endurance to many who withstand such rigors to be in the church services. And the excuses for not attending: millions of them and all different! I found what must be the favorite recipe for many folks recently. It goes like this: "Stay in bed until ten. Read Sunday paper until one. Feed your face until three. Lay around until nine. Nothing doing; nothing done. Good night!" It must be an old schedule though -- no football or baseball games in it.

William Morgan, a missionary in Brazil tells about attending church in a remote section where he serves. He drove nine hours to get there, arrived late and had to stand at the back with a group of mothers with small babies. It was cold and his feet and body ached after the long trip. It was easy to complain until, after the service of nearly three hours, the pastor's wife introduced him to some of the ladies and told him that they had walked over three hours to get to the service,. stood holding their babies during the long, long service and they would return home immediately after lunch, three hours, walking again. The missionary was certainly glad he hadn't complained aloud for his discomfort. By the way, the native ladies did not walk to just that one service, they were always faithful in attendance and they didn't even have road to follow. They had to walk through the woods.

The Psalmist said **"Let them exalt him also in the congregation of all the people"**. (Psalms 107:32) The writer of Hebrews admonished us not to forsake the assembling of ourselves together. (Hebrews 10:25) Church attendance is important for all of us, for the good it will do each of us and for the message it will give to others who know that we claim to be Christians. Have you ever stopped to think of what friends and neighbors might think about your own personal Christianity frequency and spirit of your attendance at the worship assemblies of your church?

Have you heard the little poem by Tom Olson? It goes like this:

Often when I pass a church I drop in for a visit,
So that when I'm carried in, the Lord won't say, "Who is it?"

I'm sure that every church leader has listened at one time or another to the many and varied excuses for lack of church attendance. Even many of us who attend regularly are capable of thinking up reasons why we should not have to attend.

A Lesson on Salvation

A tremendous lesson is to be learned in the 45th chapter of the book of Isaiah. The lesson concerns the ultimate power of God over all things and all persons -- all that was, all that is, and all that shall be. The chapter concerns a pronouncement of God's judgment on the frivolity and faithlessness of the people of Israel, His chosen people, and His method of freeing them from a captivity He had allowed earlier. He was to choose the Persian King Cyrus, to free them. What a blow to their pride and to their easy explanations that God preferred them! The lesson to them, and to us, was that history is a unit because there is one God and He can raise men and nations to accomplish his purpose.

Isaiah 45:5-8 contain a statement by God, "**I am the Lord, and there is none else. I form the light, and create darkness -- let the earth open, and let them bring forth salvation, and let righteousness spring up together; I the Lord created it.**" Part of the chapter is taken up with the anticipation of the people's reaction to God's using a foreign ruler to free them. And then God called their attention back to their basic need in verses 22-23, "**Look to me and be ye saved, all the ends of the earth: for I am God, and there is none else. I have sworn by myself, the word is gone out of my mouth in righteousness, and shall not return, that unto me every knee shall bow, every tongue shall swear.**"

The deliverance of the Israelites by God as pictured in this passage is a picture also of His deliverance of men throughout the ages. We look to one totally outside ourselves, to power that is not our own. The same idea is stated in Philippians 2:10-11, "**Every knee should bow, every tongue should confess that Jesus Christ is Lord**". Your own deliverance is dependent, not upon yourself, but upon Christ, an outsider to your own personality. No human being has the power within himself to overcome the temptations to sin, or to pay the penalties of sin. No human being has the power to extend his own life out into eternity, to free himself from the shackles of mortality. No human has the power to live without sin. Weakness, sinfulness, and death are inherent in every man. You may not like it that God has chosen another method besides your own works for your deliverance. You may not like it that God has chosen another person besides yourself to guide you through mortality to immortality. The point is: God is God, and God has made you, God has sustained you, and God has chosen the way of salvation for you. Isaiah 45:9 says, **"Woe unto him that striveth against his Maker!"** It only does harm to fight against God. And always remember this: God has made the way of salvation for you because he loves you.

Radical Christians?

We hear a lot of talk about radicals today as if they represent something new in the course of history. Franklin D. Roosevelt spoke of them back in 1939, when in a radio speech he said, "A radical is a man with both feet firmly planted in the air." The Bible speaks of radicals, too. Jesus spoke to the Pharisees as radicals in their practice of religion, (Matthew 23:23) when he said, "**Ye pay tithes (even) of mint and cumin.**" Paul said, in Acts 26:5, "**After the straitest sect of our religion I lived a Pharisee.**" The scribes and Pharisees were so radical in their interpretation of their religion that a minor injury could not be treated on the Sabbath, nor could a meal be cooked on that day. There were many very strict ideas, especially in relation to the day of worship.

But these are negative thoughts. On the positive side, God expects us to be radicals to an extent in our Christian experience. Romans 7:6 says, "**We should serve in newness of spirit, and not in the oldness of the letter.**" We are constantly being called to a deeper experience of belief and service in spiritual matters. There are certain things that should be a part of our daily living and Christian witness. It is absolutely necessary that we live in such a manner that people around us can tell that we are truly Christian. Jesus said, in Matthew 7:14, "**Strait is the gate and narrow is the way which leadeth unto life.**" There is a very narrow pattern into which we must fit if we are to expect to enter into eternal life, into heaven. Now, I'm not saying that we're judged on our actions; we're judged on our faith, but our faith will determine how we live, what we say and what we do. A person who truly believes that Jesus Christ died for the sins of men, that men can be saved from sin only as they believe in Christ, that men must hear the message before they can believe and that a person will be very careful to see that his life presents the message so men can grasp it and believe.

The Bible message is very narrow. Jesus is the only way into heaven, the only way of salvation. It is extremely narrow, and it takes a radical Christian to recognize and proclaim that fact. The world would water the message down, liberalize it, ease the restrictions, but it just won't work when that happens. We live in a world that tries to tell us that there is at least one exception to every rule, but in the message of God there is no exception. Every man who believes on Jesus is saved, and a man can only believe on Jesus and Him alone to be saved. I guess that makes Christians radicals but with feet firmly implanted on the Word of God.

Roosevelt, Franklin D., QuotationsBook .com/ quote /31102.

Serving Others

The writer of Hebrews has some good advice for us, today. Hebrews 13:1,2 says, **"Let brotherly love continue. Be not forgetful to entertain strangers: for thereby some have entertained angels unawares."** It's saying be nice to people, keep loving people. With some of the special problems of modern living and with some of the changed customs, it will do us well to look at this thought for a moment.

In Bible times, travelers were cared for, entertained as the passage says it, by persons in little villages and settlements along their way. There were no hotels and motels strung out along super highways as we know them today. A person was expected to take a stranger into his home to keep him for the night. It was the brotherly thing to do. He would himself be traveling sometime and would need the same help.

We are often frightened away from service like this because of some of the violence that we have seen or heard about. And, frankly, it's just not needed like it was then. But we will still have many dealings with strangers, many meetings with folks we do not know, in circumstances where we need not have fears.

The impact of the passage is that we should be careful to treat people with dignity and love, for in so doing we will find ourselves in store for many blessings we had not expected. The writer says that some have entertained angels unawares. Angels are thought of as being representatives of God, and this thought is that it is as if we were entertaining God Himself. Notice the words of Jesus in Matthew 25:34-40, **"Inasmuch as ye have done it to the least of these my brethren, ye have done it to me."** Jesus did not speak of angels here, but of charity given and love shown to persons He loved.

Be careful, now, don't run out to help someone with the wrong attitude. This entertainment of strangers is to be done in a natural way, out of a spirit of true love, the love of Christ working through you. That's why it's necessary to very carefully develop your genuine Christian personality, the one you live with 24 hours a day, 7 days a week. You can't turn on Christian brotherly love on Sunday and turn it off the rest of the week. Sorry about that!

One other quick point: More than just the blessing that will be chalked up in your favor you will find that you grow and learn when you give yourself for the good of others. The greatest 'spurts' of Christian growth I have seen in people have come when they began to go outside themselves to help others -- or "entertain strangers."

An Answer to Poverty

One of the most talked about problems of our day is termed as the poverty problem. Many are the solutions that are being tried: Marches, vigils, demands, speeches, songs, laws, and on and on the list could go. But the Psalmist had the right idea, he turned to the Lord. The 12th Psalm is a call to the Lord to help the Godly person, being the poor, who is under the oppression of the rich. Remember as you read this Psalm that if the writer is really David, as we believe him to be, then these are the words of a wealthy man petitioning God for the poor. It starts, **"Help, Lord; for the godly man ceaseth; for the faithful fall from among the children of men."** (Psalms 12:1) The idea is that there's a lot of talk about helping the poor. They speak vanity: they speak flattering words: they do a lot of double talk, as if the very talking will get the job done.

But (and here's the hope of the whole passage) when God steps in and speaks on the subject, His words are the same as action. Remember, God spoke and the world came into being, God spoke and there was light. And when God speaks to the needs of the poor, his words are vibrant with life. Verses 6 & 7 say**, "The words of the Lord are pure words: as silver tried in a furnace of earth, purified seven times. Thou shalt preserve them** (God's Words) **from this generation forever.**

There are many reasons for the poverty we know in the world of the 21st century, but the one place we must turn for help is to God! Governments, councils and investigations are not the answer. In fact, if the whole truth were known, I'm sure we would find that these may be causing more than they are curing because of the corrupt nature of men. We need to be honest enough with ourselves to recognize that some poverty will always be with us, but when we go on our knees to the Lord to ask His help in the matter, we'll find that He can step in and get a lot of things done to cure some of the sores created among us.

Of one thing I'm certain. A great deal, not all, but a great deal of the poverty we see in the world is a direct result of the Godlessness and sinfulness of persons directly affected. This has been shown many times, persons living in drunkenness and carelessness and far out of touch with God find themselves on the skids and do not stop until they are in the very pits of despair. When they are won to a saving knowledge of Jesus Christ, they begin to live seriously and gradually pull themselves up to better living.

Pray about this matter today, when God speaks He may bring action to you or through you. His Word is the only answer.

Sorrow is Better than Laughter?

The writer of the book of Ecclesiastes said a strange thing, at least in the context of our modern thought. Sorrow is better than laughter. **"For by the sadness of the countenance the heart is made better."** (Ecclesiastes 7:3). Of course, he had a good reason, for he was writing for his son to direct him away from the life of revelry and sin. He was saying that it is better to be wise and serious, even sorrowful, than to be full of laughter and be condemned.

Modern thought lays a lot of emphasis on happiness, good times, and enjoyment, but times were different in Bible days. Life was hard and dangerous. The person who would keep his life properly oriented would have to labor hard from daylight to dark, and then he would not be able to accumulate enough to took forward to any period of ease. Almost the only person who could live in ease was the thief, whether one who robbed under cover of darkness or one who used legal maneuverings. The honest man was a hard worker. The idle man was a sinner, or, at least, he was a man of suspicion.

Idleness is still a great tempter; and undue hilarity is still a sign of suspicion of weak character. A statement from James can be applied here, for he is speaking to sinners, adulterers who have made friends with the world but call themselves children of God. He says, **"Submit yourselves to God. Resist the Devil. Draw nigh to God, cleanse your hands you sinners, and purify your hearts you double minded. Be afflicted and mourn, and weep: let your laughter be turned to mourning, and your joy to heaviness."** (James 4:8-10).

You see, in this modern world with all its entertainment, and with all our idle time to enjoy that entertainment, we are tempted to try to have laughter fill our idleness; and that type of life is degrading, any way you look at it. It's the type of life that draws us away from God. Serious thinking, even times of deep sorrow and despair are often used to bring us back to God.

It's one of the great paradoxes of life, but one that I have seen to be true on many, many occasions. When a person, even an active, dependable church leader, begins to gather the tools of good times, when he begins to let recreation and entertainment take more and more of the attention that he had been giving to the things of God, then I know I will soon see him falling away from his service responsibilities, maybe completely drop out of church, or at least begin to have some difficulties in that area. It takes some serious thinking bordering on sorrow to keep things right. Give it some thought today.

We All Depend on One Another

The Psalmist wrote the words, **Behold, how good and how pleasant it is for brethren to dwell together in unity!** (Psalms 133:1). Alexander Pope wrote the little rhyme, "All are parts of one stupendous whole, Whose body nature is and God the soul." Unity is a strange word, and I'm sure that it means different things to different people, but there's a oneness in God's creation that we cannot overlook.

In this vast expanse of creation that we call the Earth, God has made every phase of life to be dependent upon all the rest, animals, plants, chemicals. Each produces for the other, each depends upon the other. And so it is in human beings. We are an interdependent lot. We must have each other.

In Acts we read, **God hath made of one blood all nations of men for to dwell on all the face of the earth.** (Acts 17:26). Paul said, **Whether one member suffer, all the members suffer with it**. (1 Corinthians 12:26). It's true of a group like a football team. It's true of a body of employees in a great manufacturing concern. It's true of the populace of a city, state, or nation. It's true of a church. It's true of the total body of believers in Christ throughout history.

Our lives are meshed together in a wondrous way so that we can give each other the uplift, the prayer support and the cooperation necessary to withstand the rigors of life in the face of the enemy. Would you believe that you have an important place in this sea of humanity, today? It's true! Don't treat it lightly.

Look at it this way. Unless this generation does something specific to hand down the message of Jesus Christ, the word of the Lord could die when we die. I know this is a far-fetched idea, but it's still one that requires some definite thinking. Every new-born child represents a new generation, a new generation that will not know Christ in personal salvation unless told by the generation passing from the scene. We picture the new year as a new babe coming into being on the first day of the new year, and the old year as an aged old man fading away at the same time. But it's not like that in real life. We have the young and we have the time to train them in the ways of God. And we have each other to love, to admonish, to help.

There is someone who cannot get along without you, today. How about that? Be to that one for good and not evil! Raise him or her up to a greater enjoyment of life, to a finer existence, because you are in your place and willing to be used by a loving God to make the world better.

Create in Me a New Heart

Do you ever try to convince yourself that you're really good at heart? Or has someone else tried to show you that all men are really good after all? It's not so! Did you know that? The Bible says that we're more naturally evil. Look at Genesis 8:21, **The imagination of man's heart is evil from his youth.** Then look at Jeremiah 17:9, **The heart is deceitful above all things, and desperately wicked**. The Bible paints a rather dismal picture of man. (That's us, friend.) Romans 3:23 adds to the idea, **All have sinned and come short of the glory of God.**

It may not be good for our ego to be told things like this, but in our own minds we know it is true. We find all our good intentions fading away into nothingness, all our grand thoughts of righteousness carried away on the four winds. At first, it's hard to take it, but gradually we are made to realize that true righteousness cannot come in man's life until he first recognizes that he cannot attain it for himself. The Psalmist cried out with all the rest of us when he said, **Create in me a new heart, 0 God and renew a right spirit within me.** (Psalms 51:10).

As each day comes and goes, and you carefully take note of the passing scene, gradually there comes an insight, a slow increase of understanding. And then it dawns! Each and every day is a separate segment of life, and the greater life shall be determined by the decision with each new day that God and God alone can make the day what it ought to be Here is the secret of life. Decision for right cannot be made once to count for all time, but decision must come each day to let God control the heart, give direction to the mind, and lay another brick of brightness to a life-a-building.

This in no way says that each day will be crowned with victory, that only smiles will be seen and never a frown. It doesn't mean that all our days will be sunny, with never a cloud to mar our sky. It means that God will give purpose to life, direction and hope, and that He will give insights along the way that will enable us to press toward the mark, the high calling to which he has called us.

In this day millions of Christians will be living and moving in millions of ways. So many lives, so many hearts, but each one with a definite place in the plan of God for the ages; each one with an attitude to be expressed; each one with a spirit to be felt. You can be one of the millions expressing an attitude of love, showing forth the spirit of Christ in your dealings with others. In its natural state your heart is evil, but God can create in you a new heart and a new spirit for this day.

You Can Do It!

We hear a lot about the idea of self-righteousness, and rightly so. One of the dangers of life is to credit ourselves for many good things when we ought to be thanking God. However, today I would like to look briefly at the opposite, what I will term as self-crucifixion. Think about 1 John 3:20, **If our heart condemn us, God is greater than our heart, and knoweth all things.** J.B. Phillips calls this idea one of the "serendipities," the happy unexpected discoveries he made when he was doing his translation of the New Testament. He says it's almost as if John is saying, "If God loves us, who are we to be so high and mighty as to refuse to love ourselves?"

Much of what we call emotional illness is the person's inability or refusal to actually love himself and give himself some credit for good. Many very capable persons, potential powerhouses for God, are doing nothing for the cause of Christ simply because they have convinced themselves that they can't, that they would stumble if they tried, that their ideas and conceptions are silly and infantile. And so, accomplishment zero!

For instance, many - very many - men in today's churches have convinced themselves that their abilities in church work are nil. Yet, in civic clubs, scout groups, and the like, they give outstanding performances. With many it's this way... "I can do this, but I can't do that." With others, there is a complete rejection of self-ability, complete self crucifixion. It's really at this point that we should apply the words of John.

Why not make a self-appraisal, today? It will do you good, especially if you are prone to degrade yourself. Remember that God loves you, has always loved you and will always love you. If He loves you, then don't you refuse to see the potential that God has created within your life. God has a purpose in all creation, including you. He hasn't made a person just to add to his toy collection, or just to be lost in the myriad of other created things. If He has built purpose into a life, then He has built the ability also into that life to see the consummation of that purpose.

This may sound like so much theory and it will be so until you take it and work it in your life. You are a wonderful creation of an almighty and loving God. He has expressed His love in your creation. He will continue to express his love in sustaining and enlarging your life, but you have to catch a glimpse of the possibilities and let Him do so.

Count Your Blessings

One of the grand old hymns we like to sing goes like this: "When upon life's billows you are tempest tossed, when you are discouraged, thinking all is lost, count your many blessings name them one by one, and it will surprise you what the Lord hath done."* And it's true, it's good for us to count our blessings. God has done so many things for us!! But this life is one of paradox. As blessings are being counted and thanks are being offered, there are many who are facing some of life's greatest trials, right now.

Here's someone with a loved one on death's bed. Here's another with one permanently disabled, another suffering the results of a tragic accident, another still mourning the recent passing of a cherished family member. All in life is not hearts and flowers, sweet and fragrant. Some of life is painful, agonizing and heartbreaking. It's easy to say that the blessings out number the hurts, that the good over balances the bad , but not always so evident for the person who is experiencing the agony today.

Let's not forget God's benefits, let's thank Him for the blessings, but let's also add our petition that God will bless by His presence and power those whom we know going through the valley of the shadow. James 5:16 says, **The effectual fervent prayer of a righteous man availeth much.** It means something when you pray for those who are suffering the ills of life. In fact, prayer is absolutely necessary. Some of the problems faced by folks you know, today, are the kind of which Jesus spoke in Mark 9:29, **This kind can come forth by nothing, but by prayer and fasting.**

It's a paradox, but it's life, on the one hand, here are blessings to count and to thank God for; and on the other hand, are pains to bear. One man suffers, another basks in the sunlight. But take it as a whole, all will suffer, all will lose loved ones, all will die. Even in our modern age of leisure, comparably good health and long life, problems and evil still are greater in most instances than are the good.

Raise up your voice in thanks. Give thanks for the many blessings you have counted that God has bestowed upon you. Let God and the world know of your gratefulness, but pray also the prayer of intercession for those who are in the throes of pain and sorrow. At the same time, give some thought to this idea. Is there some definite, concrete way that you can be used by the Lord to bring blessing in the lives of some of those in need of help? One way to express gratitude to God for blessings is to use those blessings to benefit someone else along life's way.

Hymn, "Count Your Many Blessing, is in public domain.

Real Thanks

For some reason 'thanks' is a hard word for many to say. It has always been so, and so it is today. Many of the writers of the ages have thought ill of gratitude. I suppose it's so because so much of the gratitude shown is shallow and meaningless, or maybe even a bid for more good. A French writer, (La Rochefoucauld, Maxim 298) wrote, "Gratitude in most men, is only a strong and secret hope of greater favors."

But the Thanksgiving season, in the Christian sense, reminds us that gratitude is indeed a response to be desired. Once during his ministry, Jesus healed ten lepers. Only one returned to give Him thanks, and Jesus said **Were there not ten cleansed? But where are the nine? There are none found that returned to give glory to God, save this stranger.** (Luke 17:17,18). And the scripture points out that this one who returned was a Samaritan, strongly disliked by the people of Jerusalem. The Psalmist said, **It is good thing to give thanks unto the Lord, and to sing praises unto thy name, 0 most High.** (Psalms 92:1)

If Christians really believe the Bible as we claim, then we should all realize that all good things, all life, all sustenance is given by God, that the capacity to enjoy the things of this universe has been instilled in us in the creation by God, that He has provided the balance in nature that makes life possible, that He guides us in all truth and that the assurance of salvation is ours only as God has made it possible by the exercise of His will.

No matter what the writers of the literature of the world may have said about the hypocrisy of gratitude; no matter that men all around us today have often the wrong attitude and spirit about their offered thanks, the truth remains, it is good always to give thanks to God for the immeasurable good He has done for us.

On consideration of the matter, do you find that you have been lax in giving thanks to God and to those around you for the many blessings you have enjoyed? Remember, the basic thanks go to God, for He is responsible ultimately for our blessings. But, remember, also that God uses other human beings to be his agents for good in our lives. So, in a spirit of sincere gratitude, think seriously today of the things for which you are thankful, thank God sincerely, then go and thank the person whom God used to bring the blessing to you. You don't have to be overly dramatic, just a simple, "Thank you" will do the job. Try it! You'll be glad you did!

Make a Joyful Noise

Psalm 100 is a psalm of praise, or thanksgiving, and good for our thoughts during the thanksgiving season. **Make a joyful noise before the Lord, all ye lands. 2 Serve the Lord with gladness: come before His presence with singing. 3 Know ye that the Lord He is God: it is He that hath made us, and not we ourselves; we are His people, and the sheep of His pasture. 4 Enter into His gates with thanksgiving, and into His courts with praise, be thankful unto Him and bless His name. 5 For the Lord His good; His mercy is everlasting; and His truth endureth to all generations.** (Psalms 100:1-5)

In modern language, more easily understood, the Psalm is telling us to shout out loud with intensive joy to the Lord, telling us, all of us, to let the whole earth hear our praises. In other words, there should be a certain amount of festivity in the thanksgiving praises raised by the people. We think of Christmas and Easter as being festive occasions, with thanksgiving considerably more subdued. But have you stopped to think of the fact that the thought behind the joy of these two holidays is the thanks we express? We are grateful for the birth of Jesus Christ at Christmas and for the resurrection of Jesus Christ at Easter. Thanksgiving is the time when all things are considered as we count the innumerable things that God has done for us and has given us.

This is a good time to make a point of telling others some of the many things God has done for us. I'm thinking now of the telling more than the counting. One of the great principles of Christianity is the personal witness of the Christian as he tells the world of God and His son, Jesus Christ. It is good to count your blessings, but it is also good for the world to know about them. That points to God, then, and not yourself. At the same time, it's drawing the attention of one or more persons of the world to God. You see, many in the world, today, think that any growth, improvement, gathering of wealth, or continuing good health is a result of their own study, labor and patience. Many do not stop to think that Christians really believe that God gives the blessings of life.

One of the grave needs of the world in which we live is for Christians to shout aloud so they can be heard, to shout aloud the praises to God so that unbelievers can see honest expressions of true faith. One excuse given by unbelievers is, "I just haven't seen Christians living as if they actually believe what they confess." Someone's watching, as they read between the lines of your life, what will they say?

Shout with joy before the Lord! Come before Him singing with joy. (Ps 98:4. Living Psalms).

Success Out of Struggle

Failure is an awful word a word to be feared, a word representing that something that cuts the heart out of many people. *Harry Emerson Fosdick experienced a type of failure as a young man. Of that time he said, "...shot to pieces, done in and shattered in a nervous breakdown ... all my hopes in ashes and life towering over me, saying, You are finished, you cannot, you are done for...." About that time he wrote the book, <u>The Meaning of Prayer</u>. The book, he said, came out of his struggle. He desperately needed a second chance and reinforcement to carry on with it. He was sunk unless he could find that.

Maybe to some degree you need this encouragement, today. All of us do at one time or another. Life is serious business: hard, harsh, and overbearing. Satan would like nothing better than to slam each of us to the floor and convince us that we're finished. It takes a great deal more effort to really live than we sometimes like to think.

We need to cling to the spirit of the words of Paul, **I can do all things through Christ who strengtheneth me.** (Philippians 4:13). That doesn't mean to expect total absence of failure in our lives, because none of us will cling that tightly. It does mean that we can live with an assurance that will allow us to face life, whatever the circumstances might be. It means that we can even look failure in the face without throwing up our hands and running for the nearest exit. Actually, the ultimate test of life is not how successful we have been, it's how we have tried to live it.

It's very possible that the one thing that placed Harry Emerson Fosdick in position best to be used by God was that failure, for it made the man admit that the thing he needed most, the second chance could come only from God. This is the thing that you and I need too, no matter how much success we have enjoyed or how much failure we have suffered. God needs to be the person at the wheel. He should be the one in control.

When you have let God have your life, you really don't have to be worried about whether you succeed or fail, for God gives the increase. If failure, indeed, comes, then He, God, can turn it for good and bring blessing. Remember, according to the world's standards Jesus Christ was the biggest failure in history. He claimed to be the Savior of men, but He, Himself, died on the cross of Calvary. Yet, in what the world called failure, Jesus actually performed His appointed task in eternity. Don't fear failure. Let Jesus be Lord of all you have, all you are, and all you do.

*Linn, E.H., <u>Preaching as Counseling</u>, pg 54

The Real Meaning of Love

Many are the descriptions of the thing we call love. Most of them seek to define sexual love, though, and not so much the basic quality of life that comes when we are in right relation with God. And this kind of love is what gives meaning to all human relationships. How do you express it, how do you describe it, this element of life so needed and yet so misunderstood?

Paul said it well in his letter to the Romans **Render to all their dues: tribute to whom tribute is due; custom to whom custom, fear to whom fear; honor to whom honor. Owe no man any thing, but to love one another: for he that loveth another hath fulfilled the law. For this, Thou shalt not commit adultery, Thou shalt not kill, Thou shalt not bear false witness, Thou shalt not covet; and if there be any other commandment, it is briefly comprehended in this saying, namely, Thou shalt love thy neighbor as thyself. Love worketh no ill to his neighbor: therefore love is the fulfilling of the law.** (Romans 13:7-10).

In other words, love is an all-inclusive element of life that covers the whole spectrum of our relationships with each other. If a man truly loves his neighbor, whether next door neighbor or in a distant part of the earth, real love will lead the man to such concern that he will not do a thing that will be evil toward his neighbor. When we talk about love this way, we're talking in terms of the ultimate, the infinite, the perfect. Perfect love may not be possible in human life, but it can certainly be a desired goal in life, can't it?

Jesus gave it even deeper meaning when He said, **Love your enemies, do good to them which hate you, bless them that curse**

you, and pray for them which despitefully use you. (Luke 6:27-28). That draws it down to the place where all of us live, doesn't it? It's easy to have expressions of kindness for those who are kind toward us. But to show the same spirit to those who treat us badly, that's another question all together. Let's try something today. Are you game? Put these words of Jesus to work in your life right now! How? Consider the past few days, something has happened that brought ill feeling toward someone, an intentional wrong or an accidental wrong has been committed against you. Do something good for that person. Someone has said something bad about you. You say something good about that person. Get the idea? It's not easy, but it's the real living of that which we call love.

What Does Christmas Really Mean?

What does Christmas mean? Presents for the family and friends? The sparkling eyes of children on Christmas morning when they see new toys and other goodies? Pleasant greetings from loved ones? All of these are good enough, but doesn't Christmas mean something else, too? Yes, it certainly does! It's the celebration of the Christ-child's birth, Jesus, the Christ, the Savior. Christmas means many things that could spark a deep theological discussion, but, very simply it means, **God so loved the world that he gave his only begotten son, that whosoever believeth on him should not perish, but have everlasting life.** (John 3:16). In all of the frivolity, don't forget the real background of Christmas.

You know, Jesus Christ settled a lot of the problems of men. That's right! Before his coming, men were seriously concerned with obedience of laws and with participation in religious rituals in order to attempt to keep themselves right with God. And how difficult a task that was! Every man had a different idea what God wanted!

The first murder in history was when Cain killed Abel because Abel's sacrifice was accepted by God and Cain's was not (Genesis 4). Men's hearts and minds were confused. And then there were others who didn't particularly care, just so they could make folks around them think they were righteous. All through the Old Testament are evidences that men thought material wealth and good health were signs of God's favor, God's acceptance of their religious practices.

But all of that changed with the coming of Jesus and His message, the Gospel. No longer could men put up false fronts, for now all eternity hinged upon the man's personal relationship to Jesus Christ. No longer would men do works in order to be favored by God, now they would do good works because of the love of God expressed to them through Jesus.

Don't let the loud celebration of the Christmas season this year drown out the still small voice of God, the message that lets you know how to really and truly get right with God. All the gifts you can hand out cannot buy one moment in eternity for you. All the brightly colored lights you can string around your home cannot bring a flicker of life in the vastness of eternity. Only the One whose birth we celebrate, Jesus Christ, can be effective in bringing forgiveness and everlasting life. If you don't know Him, I want you to meet Him, today. If you do already know Him, I want you to introduce Him to someone today. Let's make this genuinely a Christmas of glad tidings of great joy!

Talk Back to the Preacher

Have you ever wished you could talk back to the preacher? I'm sure you have at one time or another. Maybe you didn't quite understand what he was trying to say, or maybe you did understand but you disagreed. Dialogue is an extremely difficult thing to promote in the average church congregation, especially in a regularly scheduled church worship service where several hundred may be in attendance. Many of the New Testament gatherings were real sessions of "give and take." Some people confronted Paul one day in Athens and said, **Thou bringest certain strange things to our ears; we would know therefore what these things mean.** (Acts 18:20).

I have wondered many times, after I have delivered a message, just what the people heard as I preached. I may know what I said, but I am also aware that what I said and what the hearer understood me to say are sometimes different. I have been painfully aware, too, that many times the message I preached simply was not the message needed and expected by hearers. I can tell I didn't get tuned in to their wavelength. I heard recently of a very fine preacher and teacher who spoke several times to a great college group. According to some of the hearers, he never once touched them with what he had to say. And it's a pity, too, for college young people, of all age groups, need to hear a message, their message, from the Lord today.

One of the telltale signs of need for dialogue today is that so many of the hearers are transferring little of what the preachers say into action. Too often, people go into the church with their minds on a dozen things other than what is being said in the pulpit. And also very often, people go into the church with the predetermined idea that they are going into the service to get something, maybe comfort, but God's real message for them that day is just not comfort, therefore they 'tune out' what is being said. There are two sides to dialogue, saying something and hearing something. How nice it would be if we could always say it like its supposed to be said; and how nice it would be if we could always hear what was intended in the first place.

Would you like to join in some dialogue? You can do it by mail for phone, a comment on something I've said, a question about some statement, or some part of the message of God that you feel should be said. This might be real enjoyable for both of us. I would like to know how God impresses you through these messages.

Email: Lucian2509@gmail.com
Twitter: Twitter.com/lrudd
Facebook: Facebook.Com/lrudd4
Website: www.LucianRudd.com

The Message of Christmas

Christmas is a season of music, some of it too loud, to be sure, as it blares from the loudspeakers of the department stores across the land. But still, in all, this wonderful holiday wouldn't be the same without its music. It's interesting to see how some of the great Christmas carols have made their way into our present songfests. For instance, Isaac Watts wrote a hymn-poem based on the 98th Psalm in the early 1700's. Nearly a quarter century later, George Frederick Handel composed his great oratorio "The Messiah." But it wasn't until nearly 100 years later that, in Boston, Lowell Mason drew from Handel's "Messiah" for music appropriate to present Watt's hymn-poem. And so, we have the beautiful carol, today :

> Joy to the world! The Lord is come;
>   let earth receive her king;
> Let every heart prepare Him room,
>   and heaven and nature sing.*

The words of the Psalmist are right, **0 sing unto the Lord a new song; for he hath done marvelous things.** (Psalms 98:1). Christmas is, indeed, a time to sing. God has performed his most wonderful work ... He has given the world a Savior! It is my sincere hope that you have something to sing about this year, that you know Jesus Christ as personal Lord and Savior. If you don't, listen closely to the words of the hymns that you will hear. Maybe you will see what I mean.

    I would like to think that every Christian would be publicly acknowledging the wonder of the birth of the savior, but I know that many will get caught up in the gaiety of the season, letting many friends and acquaintances go through the entire season still wondering what it's all about.

Briefly here it is. Because of our inherent inability to live up to the standards of righteousness set out by God; He, Himself, has established a plan by which we can be forgive of our sins, by which we can have eternal life. He gave His son, Jesus Christ, to reveal to us His love, His personality, His good news. Anyone, absolutely <u>anyone</u>, who will believe on this Jesus, accept Him and His message, trust in Him, can be saved from sin for eternity. And it's the birth of this Jesus Christ we celebrate at Christmastime.

Now, sermons by the millions have been proclaimed, great songs of praise have been composed and sung, books and poems have been written, so, I know that these few moments will not suffice to tell you the whole story. Feel free to check it out. Call a church near you, today.

*Numerous resources tell the story of the origin of the hymn, "Joy to the World".

Is the Church's Message Relevant Today?

I heard some time ago of a conversation between three couples. One couple had dropped out of church completely, the second was ready to quit, and the third couple was evidently making a last-ditch effort to hold on to some of the meaning they had previously felt in the worship program of their church. The big question with all of them was the relevance of the church and its message to their lives in this modern, technological world. Change has been the by-word for the past few decades, changes in sociological patterns and changes in technology. Knowledge is increasing at a breath-taking rate. Old theories are being proven wrong. New ideas are thrown at the average citizen much faster than he can grasp them. And yet, much of the message of the church, much of the program of the church is essentially the same. And because it's the same, many people get the impression that the church can no longer relate itself to the needs of the modern man.

I suppose it is true that some of the procedures in the average church could be changed in order to better fit into the patterns of modern life, but one thing must be remembered. The Bible message is eternal, just as modern today as it was 2,000 years ago. The principles of God do not change. The sinfulness of man and his need for redemption have not been altered one whit by the onslaught of technology. In fact, we'd probably say that man's sinfulness has become even more apparent as it has become evident that he cannot morally handle the power he has discovered.

Yes, the Bible as the word of God, the church as the body of Christ and the Christian as the messenger of God do definitely have something to say to mankind today. And man needs that help, that word, more than at any other time in history because of the great power loosed in the technological advances of our age.

Paul teaches us in Ephesians 1:16-19 that God can give us the spirit of wisdom and revelation, that He can give us understanding and that He added the crowning glory to it all when he placed Jesus Christ at His right hand in the heavens. He put all things under the power of Jesus, making Him the head of the church. This Jesus who was agent of the Father in creation of all things, this Jesus who lived to give us an example of the personality of God, this Jesus who himself died on an ugly cross to pay the redemption fee for each of us, this Jesus knows also how to deal with our little everyday trivialities in life. The big thing is that you have to allow Him to do so. Open your heart to him in complete surrender and He and His message will gradually begin to become clear to you.

Stable Ground in a Changing World

Today quickly fades into history. A new day or a new decade is about to make its appearance. The old year or the old decade will be remembered for many things, one of which will be the massive changes that have been made in the technology and culture of our land. A close inventory of the changes that have actually transpired through recent years and decades are amazing. We can quickly think of things like putting men in space, along with great strides of science. There have been literally millions of new ideas that have touched the average American.

Now, change is good! Improved technology is making things easier and more enjoyable for us and I am anxious to see what new things men will discover in the years to come. But I also see a very definite need in the life of modern man for something stable and unchanging. And I believe that stability is to be found in God, in Jesus Christ, the basic personality and power behind the religion we call Christianity. Just think of it, there is hardly any part of the pattern of life that has not undergone dramatic change in this generation!

The writer of Hebrews said what we need today, **Jesus Christ, the same yesterday, and today, and for ever.** (Hebrews 13:8). He also said, **And, Thou, Lord, in the beginning hast laid the foundation of the earth; and the heavens are the works of thine hands: They shall perish; but thou remainest; and they all shall wax old as doth a garment; and as a vesture thou fold them up, and they shall be changed: but thou art the same and thy years shall not fail.** (Hebrews 1:10-12)

It seems that you and I need something to cling to, something that will give a degree of eternal security as we live in the midst of such tremendous changes. The Word of God is what we need. The Bible has the message from God for us and it's as much for us today as it was for the people of the Biblical times.

Enjoy the changes. They are a part of God's plan. New discoveries are those things which God created into the universe in the beginning, and He has allowed man to gradually accumulate the knowledge to discover these wonderful modern-day improvements.

But remember, God is still God, God is still the same God and God still expects us to respond to His call, still expects us to acknowledge the many blessings He has given us, still expects us to bow down before him in honest and sincere worship. He is the one element of all things who does not change and how glad I am! I know I can depend upon God, and I pray the same for you, also.

Jesus, Afflicted and Oppressed for Us

Isaiah 53 is one of the great mountain peaks of prophecy in the old Testament. In it is the prophet's description of God's Suffering Servant, the Messiah, a foretelling of the person of Jesus Christ.

A major thought relayed in the passage is the baring of God's own heart in suffering, a sober accounting of the price of forgiveness. The very saddest part is that so few recognized Jesus as the promised Savior of men, the personal representative of the Father in the act of redeeming sinful men. In fact, men made it harder. They brought on greater suffering. Men expected a powerful, triumphant, adventurous warrior. Instead, Jesus was God's humble and righteous servant. Because He came undramatically, like a struggling root in dry soil, who could believe that the Anointed One of God could come this way? So they rejected Him.

God's own son! Afflicted and oppressed! Yet He came to it all quietly, as a lamb to the slaughter, and the Prophet Isaiah gives us the reason behind it all. **All we like sheep have gone astray; we have turned everyone to his own way; and the Lord hath laid on him the iniquity of us all.** (Isaiah 53:6) Though we are a part of the human race, a part of the same train of mankind, God's creation, that caused the terrible agony in the heart of God and in the Suffering of Jesus Christ, though we are responsible, Jesus Christ actually lived and died to perform the work of redeeming you and me, paying the price of forgiveness for each of us.

It's really a very exciting story, and since we are so involved in it ourselves, it takes on an even more dramatic aura when we realize that this Isaiah passage is a prophecy of the suffering of Jesus Christ, given long before Christ himself was to come on the scene of history.

The basic point is this, you and I have not the power in ourselves to make ourselves right with God. We fail every time we try. The only thing we can do is depend upon the work of Jesus Christ, trust Him as Savior. That's the only way. Study the Bible regularly. It's as modern as tomorrow. It's relevant to your needs, today. This I believe with all my heart.

God Said

The Genesis account of creation tells us, **God said, Let there be light and there was light.** (Genesis 1:3) "God said." Those are significant words for us, for they convey something of the magnificent power of God. He spoke the world into existence, He spoke and there was light, He spoke and marvelous things happened. A void became beautiful Earth, full of life.

In this generation of uprisings, revolutions, and much unrest, we are prone to remind ourselves repeatedly of the so-called bad and ugly things of the world, but we need reminded of the beauty, the majesty, and the wonder of God's creation. Don't let a few of the ills of life completely dominate your thinking and hide the many good things. Remember you can take a dime and hold it close enough to your eye that you can't see anything else but the little coin, but if you hold it at arm's length, it becomes almost an insignificant object the panorama of your vision.

The pessimist allows the bad things he sees and experiences dominate him so much that he cannot think a happy thought, he cannot see a pleasant view, he cannot enjoy a happy time because he can think only of the possible evil that might transpire. Pessimism is a creeping disease of the mind that blinds the eye to good, bars the heart from joy, and closes the mind to optimistic thinking. And this pessimism is gradually creeping into the life actions of Christians and their churches. Churches are becoming accustomed to failure and Christians are losing the desire to really have a positive effect on their communities.

We need to go back to the original thought, "God said," and when God said something great power was released, victory was experienced, and great beauty came into existence. Is this still true? If it is, then we who are Christians need desperately to live as if we truly believe it. We need to be able to see and relate the beautiful things of God's universe so that others will believe also.

Listen! We need to come back again to the kind of trust that says that God can still bring about good, that God can still overcome evil, that God can still speak and cause things to happen. Maybe, in this vein, we can to be reminded of the words of Christ, **Without me ye can do nothing**. (John 15:5). We've tried to do it ourselves too long and failed too many times and so we've lost faith. Maybe we can't do it, but God can. There's still more beauty and good around us than we recognize, but also, there would be many, many more wonderful and beautiful things if we who are supposed to be God's people would really trust in Him and ask Him and expect Him to speak.

Can You Believe?

Some folks seem to have a real hard time believing. Part of the trouble is created by the very day in which we live. This is a scientific, materialistic age. Everything has to be properly verified and recorded. We are accustomed to being able to use our five senses. We want to feel, smell, taste, see, and hear; but when we come to confront God these do not suffice. It is difficult to grasp a relationship that transcends the physical.

And, too, it is hard to realize the consequences of violations in our interchanges with Him. When we violate the laws of physical interchange we can tell it right quickly. Try getting too close to a fire, try walking into a brick wall, it smarts! In spiritual matters it's different. The person who refuses to seriously consider relating himself with the Lord may not be aware of the consequences until after the end of this life. The person who is Christian but lives carelessly and commits certain sins may go years without any apparent punishment, but he will answer to God, often with serious punishment, trials and problems that God will allow. Some don't like this theology, but let's take a simple illustration. Let's say you have a child, and he does something wrong. Now, if he comes and acknowledges his wrong and asks forgiveness, what do you do? You forgive him, of course! But what if he does it again and again without any remorse or care? Eventually, you will stop him and mete out punishment, won't you? Can you expect anything really different from God? He's perfectly righteous, yes, but also perfectly just. Sin does not go unpunished whether you're Christian or non-Christian.

As I said in the beginning, some folks have a hard time believing that God really cares about how their lives are lived. Believe it, believe it, believe it! God does have some plans for your life, some ambitions in his heart for you, some restrictions on your behavior. Some things are right for you, some things are wrong for you. And, as hard as it may be to believe, God has ways to impress your mind and heart to let you know when you're right or wrong. This means that you have to trust in the fact that God is personal, just a personal as yourself. And you have to believe that you can have genuine interchange, communication, with Him. You have to believe that He can actually let you know what He expects of you. Preachers speak often of God's will for a person, that's what I'm talking about today, God's plan for you.

Do you have a hard time believing that God is really personal, powerful, and present? He is. And I pray that He will impress you today, with His presence, His power, and His personality.

Casual Christian or Deep Dedication?

What is Christianity, anyhow? The question comes hauntingly day after day. Christianity is many things to many people. Often we hear complaints about different persons because they don't live according to someone else's idea of Christianity. And I must admit that I, too, am quite often concerned because of the lack of proof of a person's professed relationship with God.

The thing that brings this to mind at this time is the casualness, the nonchalant attitude so evident in Christian circles today. With so many of us Christians, spiritual matters are something that can be taken or left, done or undone, at least for the moment.

And I believe that's the key. Spiritual improvement, religious practices, Christian services, all of these efforts involving actions are things that we want to put off till another day. Real Christian dedication is something that is reserved for the later years of life. Right now we like to think that we're "under grace' and therefore don't really have to obey any laws or show any outward proof of Christian experience.

But what did Paul say? **I beseech you therefore, brethren, by the mercies God, that ye present your bodies a living sacrifice, holy, acceptable unto God, which is your reasonable service. And be not conformed to this world: but be ye transformed by the renewing of your mind, that ye may prove what is that good, and acceptable, and perfect, will of God.** (Rom. 12:1,2)

You, see, God actually expects something constructive out of every person who has been saved by His grace. Certain standards of conduct, truth, and morality, and certain practices of worship will reflect the personality of Jesus Christ for the benefit of non-Christians. These are part of the life of every man, woman and child that expects to ever be able to enjoy that eternal happiness of residence in heaven.

There is definitely a lot of complacency among us in this day. I cannot be the judge of where the line will be drawn on the day of judgment, and neither can you. Christ himself will give the eternal answer. Some will be greatly surprised. I hope with all my heart that it won't be you! Will you spend time today to take stock of your relationship with God? If there's something about it that you've been wanting to do some day, do it today! And by the way, I'm talking to you, whether you are Christian or non-Christian. Come today into a vital, living relationship with the Lord. You won't be sorry you did.

Let No Man Take Your Crown

John 16:22 says, **Ye now therefore have sorrow, but I will see you again, and your heart shall rejoice and your heart shall be sorrowful, but your sorrow shall be turned to joy.** The Lord was telling his disciples that the shock of deep sorrow would be heavy on their shoulders for awhile, but that it would last only a short while and they would be happy again. He was speaking of a specific time, his Crucifixion followed by his resurrection and forty days of appearances, but we can also see that the truth has timeless meaning, for the disciples also had days ahead of them that would again be dark and dreary with sorrow and suffering. This same teaching fits that need, for this life is so short that any pain or sorrow will naturally be limited by the very brevity of life.

John was saying somewhat the same thing in Revelation 3:11 as he relayed the Lords message to the church at Philadelphia, **Behold, I come quickly: hold that fast which thou hast, that no man take thy crown.** He was telling the people that, as bad as the suffering and persecution might be, they should hold fast to their faith in Christ for he would be coming soon. Life is short when we compare it to the endlessness of eternity. Suffering is shallow when we compare it to the depth of the love of God we shall experience in heaven.

Now, for some this is a difficult matter. The cry is rising from many hearts to give them some of the good things of life now. Eternity seems too far away. The here and now is much to be desired over the "by and by pie in the sky." Is that how you feel today?

Look at the words of James 4:14, **For what is your life? It is even a vapor that appeareth for a little time, and then vanisheth away.**

Life may seem long to you, especially in your youth, but as the years begin to add up, it's amazing just how fast it flies by. It's like the vapor that arises from a pan of boiling water. It rises a little distance above the pan and then it disappears in the twinkling of an eye. And this thought of eternity becomes more important than we might have thought, for, you see, the experiences of eternity that you and I will have depend altogether on how we have faced today's problems. Have we fallen into deep despair or have we lifted head and heart to the Lord and expressed our faith in Him? Have we tried to live as Christ would want us to live and let Him take care of the problems?

Think about some problem you have had in the past, how big it seemed then, how it loomed as the most important thing in life at that moment. But right now it's hard to even remember all the details, isn't it? So, look up! It won't last too long! There's joy ahead when you know Jesus Christ!

Index of Scriptures

With Messages in which they were used

Acts 4:12 – Jesus, the Way, the Only Way
Acts 10:42-43 – Jesus, the Way, the Only Way
Acts 17:26 – We All Depend on One Another
Acts 18:20 – Talk Back to the Preacher
Acts 26:5 – Radical Christians
1 Corinthians 12:26 – We All Depend on One Another
1 Corinthians 13:3 – Helping Others
Ecclesiastes 7:3 – Sorrow is Better than Laughter?
Ephesians 1: 16-19 – Is the Church's Message Relevant Today?
Ephesians 5:2, 8,15 – Walking Before God
Ephesians 5:15-16 – Redeeming the Time
Ephesians 6:14 – Stand Up for Jesus
Genesis 1:3 – God Said
Genesis 8:21 – Create in Me a New Heart
Genesis 17:1 – Walking Before God
Hebrews 1:10-12 – Stable Ground in a Changing World
Hebrews 10:25 – See You in Church?
Hebrews 13:1-2 – Serving Others
Hebrews 13:8 – Stable Ground in a Changing World
Isaiah 12:3 – A Joy to Shout About
Isaiah 41:20 – Hurry Up!

Isaiah 45:5-8, 22-23 – A Lesson on Salvation
Isaiah 45:9 – A Lesson on Salvation
Isaiah 53:6 – Jesus, Afflicted and oppressed for Us
James 4:8-10 – Sorrow is Better than Laughter?
James 4:14 – Let No Man Take Your Corwn
James 5:16 – Count Your Blessings
Jeremiah 17:9 – Create in Me a New Heart
Job 37:14 – Hurry Up
John 3:16 – What Does Christmas Really Mean?
John 5:8 – Walking Before God
John 14:6 – Jesus, the Way, the Only Way
John 15:5 – God Said
John 15:11 – A Joy to Shout About
John 15:13 – A Living Sacrifice
John 16:22 – Let No Man Take Your Crown`
1 John 3:20 – You Can Do It
Judges 5:31 – Shining Sun Christian
Leviticus 26:12 – Walking Before God
Luke 6:27-28 – The Real Meaning of Love
Luke 16:8 – Redeeming the Time
Luke 17:17-18 – Real Thanks
Mark 9:29 – Count Your Blessings
Matthew 7:14 – Radical Christians
Matthew 14:25 – Walking Before God
Matthew 23:23 – Radical Christians
Matthew 25:34-40 – Serving Others
Matthew 25:41-46 – Helping Others
Numbers 10:29 – We Can Do You Good!
Philippians 2:10-11 – A Lesson on Salvation
Philippians 2:15 – Shining Sun Christian
Philippians 4:3 – Success Out of Struggle

Proverbs 16:20 – Light For Life
Proverbs 22:3 – Redeeming the Time
Proverbs 22:16 – Train Up the Child
Proverbs 26:20 – Words Can Hurt
Psalms 3:5 – Light For Life
Psalms 12:1, 6-7 – An Answer to Poverty
Psalms 51:10 – Create in Me a New Heart
Psalms 92:1 – Real Thanks
Psalms 94:17 – Light For Life
Psalms 98:1 – The Message of Christmas
Psalms 98:4 – Make a Joyful Noise
Psalms 100:1-5 – Make a Joyful Noise
Psalms 107:32 – See You in Church?
Psalms 112:2 – Got Enough Excitement?
Psalms 133:1 – We All Depend on One Another
Revelation 3:11 – Let No Man Take Your Crown
Romans 3:23 – Create in Me a New Heart
Romans 7:6 – Radical Christians
Romans 12:1 – A Living Sacrifice
Romans 12:1-2 – Casual Christian or Deep Conviction?
Romans 13:7-10 – The Real Meaning of Love

**Now to Him who is able
to do exceedingly
abundantly
above all that we ask or think,
according to the power
that works in us,
to Him be glory in the church
by Christ Jesus
throughout all ages,
world without end.
Amen**
Ephesians 3:20,21

Notes

Notes

Notes

Notes

Notes

Notes

Notes

Notes

Notes

Notes